Ireland

The Revolutionary Years

Ireland
The Revolutionary Years

Photographs from the Cashman Collection
Ireland 1910-30

Edited by Louis McRedmond

Gill and Macmillan & Radio Telefís Éireann

Published by

Gill and Macmillan Ltd

Goldenbridge

Dublin 8

and

Radio Telefís Éireann

Donnybrook

Dublin 4

Text © Louis McRedmond 1992

Photos © The Estate of the late Joseph Cashman 1992

Designed by Mark Loughran

Print origination by Seton Music Graphics Ltd, Bantry, Co Cork

Printed in Hong Kong

BRITISH LIBRARY CATALOGUING-IN-PUBLICATION DATA

Ireland: the revolutionary years:

Photographs from the Cashman Collection: Ireland 1910-30.

I. McRedmond, Louis

941.7082022

ISBN 0-7171-1710-3

P R E F A C E

J oseph Cashman, the photographer whose work is celebrated in this book, was born in Blackrock, County Cork in 1881. From his earliest years, he was fascinated by cameras and photography. Later in life, he could recall himself as a boy of ten or eleven staring at cameras - still expensive, new-fangled things in those days - in shop windows on Patrick Street. While still in his teens he went to work for the first time, at the famous Cork printing house of Guy and Co. After a few years he joined the Cork Examiner, thus beginning an association with newspapers that was to last all his life. He worked as a photo engraver and photographer for the Examiner during the first decade of the new century, although he also spent a couple of years in Wales with the Cambria Daily Leader. By 1911 he was in Dublin, in charge of the photo engraving department of the Freeman's Journal.

All the time, he had continued his own work and had developed into a photographer of rare documentary ability, as the photographs in this book testify. It is no exaggeration to say that in the period 1910 -30 he was probably the most influential single recorder of public events in Ireland, at the time when the country was convulsed by revolutionary changes.

*A*lthough never a member of any political party, Joseph Cashman was a socialist by conviction and an early follower of James Larkin. His famous photograph of an impassioned Larkin addressing a crowd in O'Connell Street is one of the enduring images of twentieth-century Ireland. It lives not only in photographic form but also in stone: it was the model for Oisín Kelly's statue of Larkin which now stands in O'Connell Street, close to the spot where the original speech was delivered.

The Freeman's Journal ceased publication in 1923. Cashman was now sufficiently well established as a photographer to set up his own studio at 21 Capel Street, where he quickly built up a thriving business, specialising in bloodstock photography. Inevitably, his documentary output fell in this period.

In 1929, he received a letter from Éamon de Valera asking him to set up and manage both the photographic and photo engraving departments in the new newspaper which Fianna Fáil was about to launch. He took up this offer enthusiastically. He was, in effect, the founding father of photography in the Irish Press. He bought the machinery he needed in London; he organised and managed both departments; and he oversaw the work of builders, so that the physical layout of his departments was to his satisfaction. In these matters, as in everything he did, he was a perfectionist.

*H*e maintained his own studio up to the end of the war
and continued to take photographs until the mid fifties.
After that, there was very little, although, as the final images in
this book demonstrate, he was still capable of capturing a scene
with wit and precision in his mid eighties.

Joseph Cashman died in January 1969 at the age of 87.

In 1913 the leader of nationalist Ireland was John Redmond, who had loyally stood by Parnell at the time of the split in the Irish Party. He reunited the Party and skilfully secured the passage of the Home Rule Bill at Westminster which provided for government of the country by an Irish parliament.

The outbreak of the Great War in August 1914 delayed the introduction of Home Rule and support for Redmond declined rapidly under the pressure of events at home and abroad in the following four years.

After a lifetime of dedicated service to his country he died in March 1918 and was buried in the family vault in Wexford. With him died the lingering hope that the Irish Question might be settled by purely parliamentary means.

The ragged and barefoot children of Dublin, here playing at soldiers, illustrate the shocking social conditions which culminated in the strike of 1913 followed by the lock-out imposed by a combination of city employers to break the trade union movement led by Jim Larkin (overleaf, photographed in 1923 on his return to Dublin from the United States) and James Connolly (overleaf).

When Larkin attempted to address workers and passers-by from an hotel window in O'Connell Street (then known as Sackville Street) on Sunday 31 August 1913 the police baton-charged the crowd, causing many injuries.

*I*n Ireland as in other countries women were demanding the right to vote and a suffragette was arrested for protesting at the Mansion House in Dublin. A champion of the feminists, Francis Sheehy Skeffington (below, right), was also concerned to find some way of protecting the workers against attacks like the August baton charge. Together with Captain White, D.S.O. (below, left), he helped Connolly set up the Irish Citizen Army.

*T*he Irish National Volunteers, founded in November 1913, became a bigger organisation; they were a response to the Ulster Volunteer Force, which had been formed to resist implementation of Home Rule in the North. At first the Irish National Volunteers had no arms, as could be seen when they marched through Ranelagh, Dublin.

*T*he Volunteers were not unarmed for long. Erskine Childers brought guns from Germany on his yacht Asgard and landed them at Howth pier in July 1914.

Bystanders cheered as the guns were driven away and the Volunteers soon began to look more like soldiers.

*R*edmond urged the Volunteers to join the British army in the
Great War, both to show solidarity with small countries like
Belgium and Serbia which had been invaded and to prove
that a Home Rule Ireland would be friendly to Great
Britain. Enthusiastic crowds attended his recruiting rallies in
Wexford and elsewhere.

A small minority of the Volunteers disagreed with
Redmond and broke away from the main body. The
dissidents became known as the Irish Volunteers
(sometimes, incorrectly, the Sinn Fein Volunteers); the rest
as the National Volunteers.

Redmond and his party colleague, 'Wee Joe' Devlin
from Belfast, went to the Phoenix Park in 1915 for a parade
of National Volunteers (above) who had enlisted in the
army but Redmond's position was now being undermined
from other quarters than the breakaway element.

The Unionist leader, Sir Edward Carson, became a
member of the British government in June 1915 and this
raised nationalist fears that all or part of Ulster would be
allowed to opt out of Home Rule.

M eanwhile, the old regime continued. The Earl of Aberdeen had been Lord Lieutenant for ten years when he and his wife were photographed in 1915 and Lady Aberdeen continued to attend school prizegivings.

Lord Wimborne, a cousin of Winston Churchill, succeeded Aberdeen as Lord Lieutenant in 1915. Many thousands of Irishmen had joined the army in the first year of the war and Wimborne inspected the troops at Dublin Castle (opposite). The police put on a spirited Trooping the Colour in the Castle Yard (opposite).

POBLACHT NA H EIREANN.

THE PROVISIONAL GOVERNMENT
OF THE
IRISH REPUBLIC
TO THE PEOPLE OF IRELAND.

IRISHMEN AND IRISHWOMEN : In the name of God and of the dead generations from which she receives her old tradition of nationhood, Ireland, through us, summons her children to her flag and strikes for her freedom.

Having organised and trained her manhood through her secret revolutionary organisation, the Irish Republican Brotherhood, and through her open military organisations, the Irish Volunteers and the Irish Citizen Army, having patiently perfected her discipline, having resolutely waited for the right moment to reveal itself, she now seizes that moment, and, supported by her exiled children in America and by gallant allies in Europe, but relying in the first on her own strength, she strikes in full confidence of victory.

We declare the right of the people of Ireland to the ownership of Ireland, and to the unfettered control of Irish destinies, to be sovereign and indefeasible. The long usurpation of that right by a foreign people and government has not extinguished the right, nor can it ever be extinguished except by the destruction of the Irish people. In every generation the Irish people have asserted their right to national freedom and sovereignty ; six times during the past three hundred years they have asserted it in arms. Standing on that fundamental right and again asserting it in arms in the face of the world, we hereby proclaim the Irish Republic as a Sovereign Independent State, and we pledge our lives and the lives of our comrades-in-arms to the cause of its freedom, of its welfare, and of its exaltation among the nations.

The Irish Republic is entitled to, and hereby claims, the allegiance of every Irishman and Irishwoman. The Republic guarantees religious and civil liberty, equal rights and equal opportunities to all its citizens, and declares its resolve to pursue the happiness and prosperity of the whole nation and of all its parts, cherishing all the children of the nation equally, and oblivious of the differences carefully fostered by an alien government, which have divided a minority from the majority in the past.

Until our arms have brought the opportune moment for the establishment of a permanent National Government, representative of the whole people of Ireland and elected by the suffrages of all her men and women, the Provisional Government, hereby constituted, will administer the civil and military affairs of the Republic in trust for the people.

We place the cause of the Irish Republic under the protection of the Most High God, Whose blessing we invoke upon our arms, and we pray that no one who serves that cause will dishonour it by cowardice, inhumanity, or rapine. In this supreme hour the Irish nation must, by its valour and discipline and by the readiness of its children to sacrifice themselves for the common good, prove itself worthy of the august destiny to which it is called.

Signed on Behalf of the Provisional Government,

THOMAS J. CLARKE,

SEAN Mac DIARMADA,   THOMAS MacDONAGH,

P. H. PEARSE,   EAMONN CEANNT,

JAMES CONNOLLY.   JOSEPH PLUNKETT.

*I*n defiance of an order from their Chief of Staff, Professor Eoin Mac Neill, a section of the Irish Volunteers under the command of Patrick Pearse as Commandant-General, together with the Citizen Army under Connolly, occupied a number of buildings in Dublin on Easter Monday 1916.

The decision to act was taken by a clandestine organisation, the Irish Republican Brotherhood; the Irish Volunteers had arguably from the beginning been an I.R.B. front. The insurgents proclaimed a Republic and set up a Provisional Government (opposite).

*P*earse made the General Post Office in O'Connell Street his headquarters. Within hours they came under attack from British forces, who included many Irish soldiers, and found themselves besieged. No photographs exist of the interior of the G.P.O. during the Rising but a romanticised painting published later (overleaf) showed the wounded Connolly still receiving reports and giving instructions, while Pearse and his brother Willie stood beside him; other signatories of the Proclamation were also included, among them Tom Clarke, Seán Mac Diarmada and Joseph Plunkett.

A British soldier took this famous snapshot of Patrick Pearse surrendering to Brigadier-General W. H. M. Lowe on the Saturday of Easter Week. Unlike some other officers, Lowe was 'courteous and paternal' (Desmond Ryan) in making arrangements for the surrender with Pearse's representative, Nurse Elizabeth O'Farrell, who cannot be seen standing beyond Pearse but whose billowing skirt creates the impression in the blurred picture that the Commandant-General is wearing an overcoat. The officer with General Lowe is his son, who later became a film-maker under the name John Loder.

*T*he Volunteers were made prisoner and marched away from their various strongholds. Eamon de Valera (above, marked 'X') led his men from Boland's Mills.

*O*thers were taken down Eden Quay (right) while Dick Donahoe and Tom Doyle from Enniscorthy were brought under escort to Kilmainham Jail (above).

The prisoners were first held in various military barracks around Dublin. Among them were George and Jack Plunkett, younger brothers of Joseph Plunkett, the poet who was executed as one of the leaders of the Rising. They were condemned to death but later reprieved. 'A press photo shows them in their Volunteer uniforms, looking like schoolboys on a Scout outing, remarkably cheerful,' wrote their niece, the novelist Eilis Dillon.

*J*oseph Plunkett was engaged to be married to Grace Gifford and the British authorities permitted the wedding to be held by candle light in the chapel of Kilmainham Jail on the evening before Plunkett's execution; two soldiers were the official witnesses.

Plunkett had then to return to his cell but his wife was allowed visit him briefly on the following morning in the presence of armed guards before he was taken away to be shot.

Plunkett's parents, the Count and Countess Plunkett, were photographed some time later with their daughter-in-law.

*A*fter condemnation by courts martial set up by the Commander-in-Chief of the British forces in Ireland, General Sir John Maxwell, fourteen participants in the Rising, including Pearse and Connolly, were executed by firing squad here in the Stonebreakers' Yard of Kilmainham Jail between 3 May and 12 May 1916. (Tom Kent was executed in Cork and Roger Casement, later, in London, bringing the total to the sixteen honoured by Yeats in a famous poem.)

*M*axwell later reviewed the older soldiers of the reserve corps known in Dublin as the 'Gorgeous Wrecks' (from the 'Georgius Rex' device on their armbands) in the grounds of Trinity College; they had suffered a number of casualties in the fighting on Easter Monday.

*T*he destruction of many
buildings in Dublin
(see also overleaf),
including the Liberty
Hall headquarters of
Connolly's Union and
the Citizen Army, was
brought about by
British artillery during
Easter Week but the
people at first blamed
the Volunteers for
provoking the shellfire.

A novelty in the streets of Dublin in 1916 was a lorry converted into an armoured car. The Fire Brigade had a major job on its hands, especially as it was not allowed to deal with any of the fires in the city until the Saturday of Easter Week.

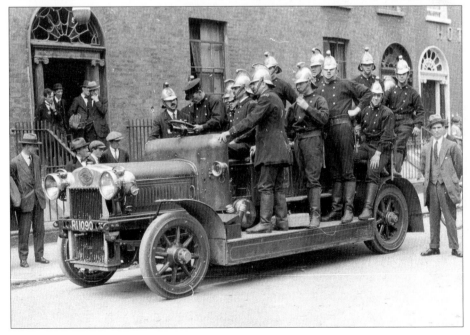

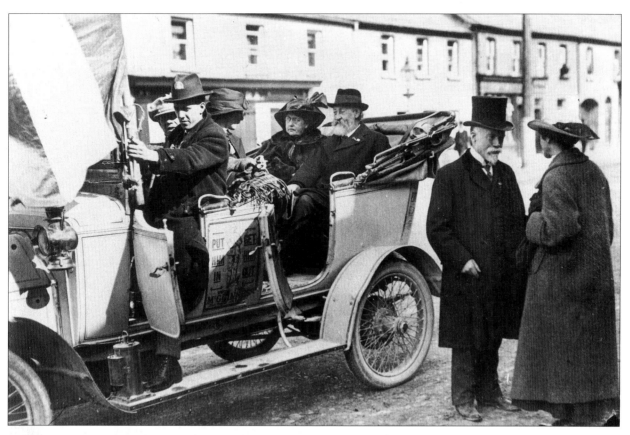

*D*espite the initial unpopularity of the Rising at a time when so many Irishmen were serving in the Great War, the insurgents were felt to have put up a good fight and the executions were considered outrageously vindictive. So was the continuing detention in Britain of many of the Easter Week prisoners. Count Plunkett received twice as many votes as the Redmondite candidate at a by-election in North Roscommon in February 1917.

The Count and his wife (in car) went on in May to campaign for Joe MacGuinness, still a prisoner in England, who had been nominated by Sinn Fein at a by-election in Longford under the slogan 'Put him in to get him out.' MacGuinness won. There could be little doubt now which way the wind was blowing, notwithstanding the brave front maintained by Irish Party supporters.

*T*he release of prisoners held
without trial in Britain since
the Rising caused little stir in
December 1916.

Some 120 prisoners
who had been sentenced by
courts martial were not
released until June 1917.

They met a very
different reception, indicative
of the rapidly changing mood
of the country. Crowds
waving the tricolour greeted
them at Westland Row station
in Dublin and a special
welcome awaited the
Countess Markievicz of the
Citizen Army at Liberty Hall.

*F*urther by-elections were won by the 1916 veterans, Éamon de Valera and William T. Cosgrave (left and right respectively). De Valera, already elected for Clare, spoke on behalf of Cosgrave in Kilkenny. The militants were now grouped within the constitutional Sinn Fein party of Arthur Griffith, which favoured the election of M.P.s who would refuse to attend Westminster and instead form themselves into an Irish parliament.

*F*eeling was now running so high that at Kilkenny the Irish Party had to have police protection and suffer the taunts of Sinn Feiners waving the tricolour.

Redmond made one last attempt to resolve the Irish crisis by agreement but the Convention of nationalists, unionists and other interests which met in Trinity College was denounced by Sinn Fein and failed to establish common ground between nationalists and Ulster unionists.

Meanwhile, Sinn Feiners were being arrested for seditious speech-making and illegal drilling. Some protested by going on hunger strike. Forced feeding brought about the death of Thomas Ashe, whose funeral on 30 September 1917 was made the occasion for a huge national demonstration by Volunteers, trade unions and the people of Dublin. Among the 150 clergy who attended were the Capuchin Fathers Albert and Augustine, and (centre) the Benedictine Dom Francis Sweetman.

One issue on which all nationalists were able
to agree was resistance to the conscription
of Irishmen into the British army,
proposed in April 1918.

    In these photographs, de Valera is
shown about to address an anti-
conscription meeting at Ballaghaderreen,
where he shared the platform with John
Dillon (with white beard, seated beside
de Valera, right) who had succeeded
Redmond as leader of the Irish Party.

    Protests against conscription were
recorded at church gates throughout
the country.

P rominent personalities of the day included Thomas Johnson, who helped organise trade union opposition to conscription and would become the first parliamentary leader of the Labour Party, and Arthur Griffith, the founder of Sinn Fein who was imprisoned after the 1916 Rising although he took no part in it; Griffith was elected member of parliament for East Cavan at a by-election in 1918.

A group photographed at Croke Park in 1918 included (left to right) a future Free State Minister, J. J. Walsh, the Countess Markievicz who would soon become the first woman to be elected to the parliament at Westminster (in which she refused to sit) and Harry Boland, a close friend and colleague of Michael Collins.

At the General Election held throughout the United Kingdom in December 1918, Sinn Fein won 73 of the 105 Irish seats. Except in Ulster, the result was a landslide. Those of the Sinn Fein members who were not in prison met in the Mansion House, Dublin, on 21 January 1919 and proclaimed themselves the parliament of the Irish Republic under the name Dail Eireann (Assembly of Ireland). They were no longer to be known as members of parliament but as Teachtai Dála or Dail Deputies (T.D.s). They elected a five-member government, to be led by Cathal Brugha for the time being instead of de Valera, who had been rearrested and was imprisoned in England.

F ollowing a dramatic escape from Lincoln Jail in February
(engineered by Michael Collins and Harry Boland) and a
British amnesty of prisoners a month later, de Valera was
able to assume his role as President of the Dail government.
His public appearances included attendance at Croke Park
to throw in the ball at a match on 6 April 1919.

Among Sinn Fein delegations which came to Dublin
for discussions in 1919 was one from Cork on which were
Tomás Mac Curtain (seated, centre) and Terence
McSwiney (standing, second from right); each in turn
would die a violent death while Lord Mayor of the city.

*I*n June de Valera went to the United States, where he remained for eighteen months, to promote support for the Republic. He met the New York State Federation of Labor Committee at Syracuse, N.Y., in August (above).

The Irish Parliamentary Party under Dillon and Devlin (left) was now a spent force except in Waterford city and in the northern part of the country, where 'Wee Joe' could attract a good attendance at a meeting in Blackrock, County Louth (below).

*N*otwithstanding all that had happened, people turned out in their thousands for the Dublin Victory Parade in August 1919 to mark the end of the Great War.

*1*919 was in fact a year of ambivalence in Irish nationalist attitudes. A campaign against policemen, which involved shooting members of the Royal Irish Constabulary (the R.I.C.) and attacking isolated barracks, had been undertaken by the Volunteers — now increasingly called the Irish Republican Army. These activities were at first widely condemned. The British response of curfews, searches and indiscriminate arrests, however, provoked much resentment. The attempted suppression of Dail Eireann and of Sinn Fein further antagonised the people who felt that their demand for independence, legitimately expressed at the polls, was being treated with contempt.

*E*motions ran high when, after a policeman had been killed in Cork, gunmen assumed to be from the Crown forces shot dead the Sinn Fein Lord Mayor, Tomás Mac Curtain, in March 1920.

Volunteers mounted a guard of honour by his coffin in Cork Cathedral before his funeral, which was attended by the Lord Mayor of Dublin, Larry O'Neill, and Arthur Griffith (in front, second from right and right, respectively).

M ountjoy Jail in Dublin became the focal point for protests by women, children and other friends and relatives of Sinn Fein prisoners who found ingenious means to wave their greetings. British military had to use heavy armour to bring convoys into the prison and sometimes had to mount cordons to hold back the crowds (this and two following pages).

*E*arly in 1920 men recruited in Britain and Northern Ireland to
serve in the Royal Irish Constabulary began to arrive and were
soon called the 'Black and Tans' (after a famous pack of
foxhounds in County Tipperary) because of the mixture of
police and army uniforms which they wore.

In July an Auxiliary Division of the R.I.C. was formed of
ex-army officers. 'Tans' and 'Auxiliaries' worked together in
units, like this one in Cork, formed to hunt down the I.R.A.

The Black and Tans were notoriously indisciplined. When they raided Liberty Hall, they made off with band equipment. In Trim, County Meath, they smashed furniture when raiding private houses.

On the night after an R.I.C. Head Constable had been shot at Balbriggan, County Dublin, lorryloads of Black and Tans arrived in the town, set fire to many shops and houses and bayonetted two local men — a dairyman and a barber — to death. People fled the town for fear of further attacks (below) but returned for their neighbours' funerals (right).

Balbriggan, as the Black and Tans left it in September 1920.

*B*y failing to listen to moderate nationalist opinion, by neglecting to respond imaginatively to
the result of the 1918 Election and by permitting large segments of the population to be
terrorised in the name of law and order, the British government played into the hands of
Sinn Fein and of Michael Collins, who directed the Volunteers' campaign to destabilise
the British administration with brilliant efficiency. By the end of 1920 it was difficult
in nationalist Ireland to avoid the impression that Britain was making war on the Irish
people, for more and more of whom there was only one side to choose. In these
circumstances, they demanded to be treated as honourable adversaries. Much anger was
evident throughout the country when a young medical student, Kevin Barry, was hanged for his
part in an ambush at Church Street, Dublin, in which a British soldier was killed (a photograph taken just after the event).

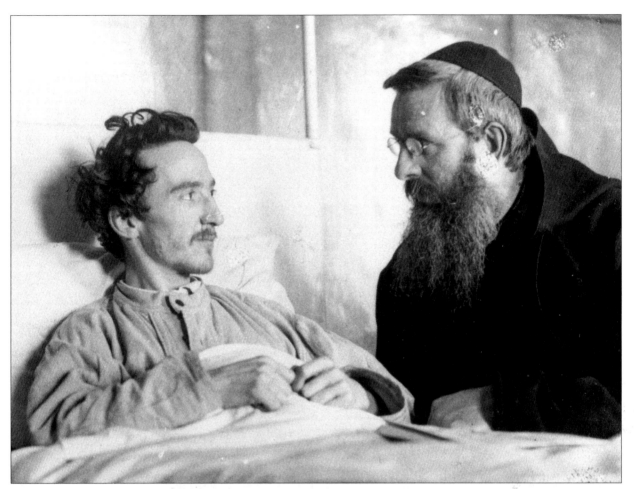

*P*risoners resorted again to hunger strikes. Father Augustine visited Cathal O'Shannon in the Mater Hospital, to which hunger strikers were now transferred from Mountjoy Jail when they became excessively weak.

*T*he most famous hunger strike was that of Terence MacSwiney, Lord Mayor of Cork, who died in Brixton Prison, London, after 74 days of fasting. The boat bringing home his remains docked at Queenstown and the coffin was taken by land to the city where the Bishop of Cork, Dr Daniel Cohalan, awaited it.

I nexorably, nationalist attitudes continued to change. The
pressure for constitutional reform had been replaced by a
demand for unequivocal independence. To this now was
added a growing sense that British authority in Ireland was
illegitimate and that the country was under illegal occupation.
Official reaction to the shootings and other activities of the
I.R.A. gave credibility to this view. Military patrols,
armoured vehicles and reinforcements rushing to scenes of
'incidents' became common in the heart of Dublin. Only an
inquisitive small boy would dare to breach a cordon.

*N*obody was immune from being stopped, questioned or searched: a pedestrian, a cyclist, the driver of an elegant motor-car (opposite), a carter (opposite), even the Post Office van (opposite).

*T*he Labour leader, Thomas Johnson, and a colleague were arrested in a raid on Liberty Hall. Taking a tricolour down from a lamp-post was the least of the duties of the army. When an armoured car broke down outside the Bank of Ireland it had to be put under heavy guard.

*W*hen soldiers put a barricade across the roadway at Summerhill in Dublin while making an arms search, the people could not leave the area. An enterprising shopkeeper set up a bread counter and sold loaves across the barbed wire.

omen and children continued to gather outside Mountjoy Jail to show their sympathy with the hunger strikers.

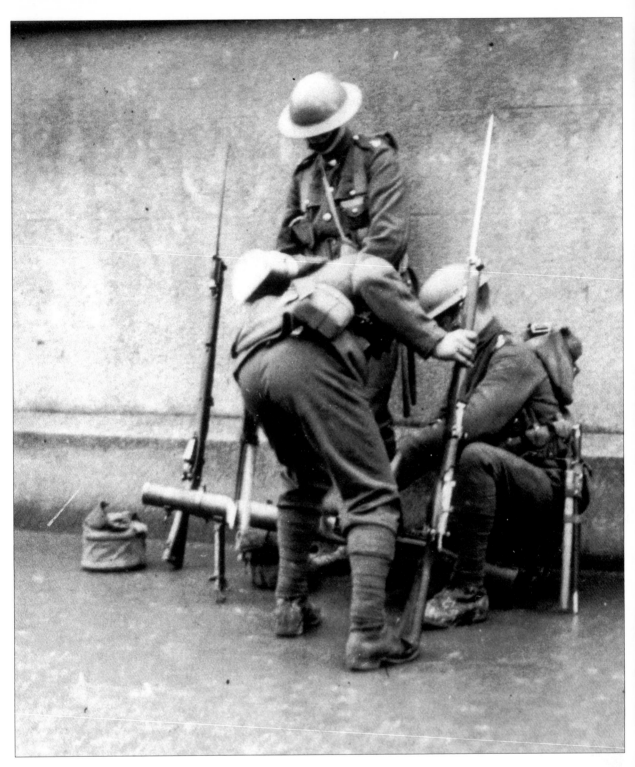

S oldiers assembled a machine-gun under the prison walls.

People kept a vigil at one entrance bringing religious

symbols with them (opposite).

As 'The Troubles' worsened, new men took charge of the British administration in Ireland. General Sir Nevil Macready became Commander-in-Chief in 1920: he is seen here with Lord French (on his right) who had been Lord Lieutenant since 1918. Sir Hamar Greenwood also arrived in 1920 as Chief Secretary — the Cabinet Minister with responsibility for Ireland. French was photographed reviewing the Black and Tans, and Macready when presenting an award to a Dublin Castle detective.

Óglaiġ na h-Éireann.

Árd-Oifiġ, Áṫ Cliaṫ.

General Headquarters, Dublin.

Department...........................

Reference No...........................

9th. July, 1921.

To:
Officers Commanding All Units.

In view of the conversations now being entered
into by our Government with the Government of Great
Britain, and in pursuance of mutual understandings
to suspend hostilities during these conversations,
active operations by our troops will be suspended
as from Noon Monday July, Eleventh.

C/S.

*I*n July 1921 came the momentous news that a truce had been agreed between the Crown forces and the Volunteers to enable negotiations to take place between the British government and representatives of the Irish government established by the Dail. Instructions issued from the headquarters of Óglaigh na h-Éireann (the Irish Volunteers) ordering the suspension of hostilities.

The Truce made it possible for Irish public figures recently at risk of arrest to appear in public. Éamon de Valera, who had returned from the United States six months previously, was able to function not only as President but also as Chancellor of the National University of Ireland (right, with the President of University College, Dublin, Dr Denis J. Coffey). He was the only person nominated for the Chancellorship in July — a further indication of the mood of the country — and he was therefore invited to undertake his duties at once although the formal election did not take place until December.

In the same month the Countess Markievicz (with Mrs Pearse, mother of Patrick and William, in right foreground) laid a wreath at the grave of the eighteenth century United Irishman and republican, Wolfe Tone.

*T*he negotiations in London were prolonged. De Valera himself had talks with the Prime Minister, Lloyd George, during the initial stages but the members of the Irish delegation for the later discussions were Robert Barton, Arthur Griffith, Edmund Duggan, George Gavan Duffy (left to right respectively) and Michael Collins.

Collins (right) disliked being photographed during the Truce, fearing that the negotiations might fail and the fighting be resumed, in which case it would be undesirable that he should be easily recognised. He grew a moustache and in one of the few pictures from this time was seen at a hurling match in Croke Park.

*T*he Anglo-Irish Treaty was signed on 6 December 1921. It proposed to establish the Irish Free State as a fully self-governing Dominion of the British Empire but effectively excluded the six counties of Northern Ireland. Northern Ireland remained within the United Kingdom although it had a government of its own with limited powers under the Government of Ireland Act, 1920. The Treaty also required T.D.s to take an oath of allegiance to the British monarch. After a bitter debate in the Dail, the Treaty was ratified by 64 votes to 57. De Valera voted with the minority who argued that the Treaty amounted to a repudiation of the Republic. He resigned as President of the Dail. Griffith succeeded him.

A complex situation followed the approval of the Treaty, with the Dail government (the government of the Republic) parallelling the Provisional Government of the Irish Free State, which was due to become the sole government within one year from the signature of the Treaty. In practice, both governments had substantially the same membership but it was on Collins as chairman of the Provisional Government that responsibility fell for on-going relations with Britain.

In February 1922 Sir James Craig, Prime Minister of Northern Ireland, came to Dublin to discuss a modus vivendi with Collins. The situation in the North had become very serious with the Unionist militia ('A Specials' and 'B Specials') attacking nationalists and being attacked in turn by the I.R.A., while the British army manned barricades in Belfast.

A mong the first tasks facing Collins was the formation of a national army. Its nucleus and its senior officer corps already existed in the I.R.A. and ensured that Free State soldiers in their green uniforms would soon become a familiar sight. But the I.R.A. was deeply divided over the Treaty. Many of its members withheld their allegiance from the Provisional Government and refused to join its army despite the vote in favour of the Treaty by a clear majority of deputies in the Dail. The rift between old comrades caused much anguish, not least to Collins.

Among those who tried to mend the breach were pro-Treaty General Seán Mac Eoin, who had been I.R.A. leader in County Longford, and his friend Seán Moylan, an anti-Treatyite I.R.A. officer from County Cork.

63

*H*urling and Gaelic football matches at Croke Park continued to provide some relief for politicians caught in a web of uncertainty. The famous Tipperary I.R.A. fighter, anti-Treatyite Dan Breen, threw in the ball early in 1922. Arthur Griffith (at far right) used to go there with J. J. Walsh, Mrs Griffith and Mrs Walsh (left to right respectively). So did Harry Boland, who opposed his friend Michael Collins on the Treaty.

*T*he complicated business of transferring control from British to Irish authorities would take the better part of a year.

I.R.A. prisoners were released from internment in the Curragh. Many joined the Free State army being formed by Collins. British soldiers meanwhile packed their belongings, from chairs and buckets to chamber pots (opposite), as they prepared to leave their many installations around the country.

*E*verywhere for
months could be
heard the tramp of
marching men: the
British marching
out, the Irish
marching in
(opposite).

*R*ecruits for the Free State forces marching up from the country. Not everybody was left to march once the Free State acquired its own armoured cars. One of them (above) was called after Michael Collins by his nickname, 'The Big Fella'.

The handing over of premises from British to Irish forces was done with dignity and correct military protocol. On a wet and blustery day in May the Irish General J. J. 'Ginger' O'Connell (left) was received by British officers at the Curragh Camp in County Kildare.

Free State soldiers raised the tricolour above the high water tower of the Camp.

Their officers saluted.

I n Dublin, General Richard Mulcahy, as Minister for Defence, together with General Eoin O'Duffy (in civilian dress) attended the installation of the colours at Beggars Bush Barracks. General O'Duffy also took the salute at Portobello Barracks with General Emmet Dalton on O'Duffy's left. When the Irish army took over responsibility for protecting the Bank of Ireland it was a symbolic as well as practical step since the Bank occupied the houses of the eighteenth century Irish Parliament suppressed by the Act of Union.

*N*othing had more symbolic significance for the new State than the handing over of Dublin Castle, seat of English (later British) administration in Ireland for 700 years, which had formally taken place in January.

Free State forces, however, were not yet ready to establish themselves there and it was only on 17 August that the last R.I.C. men made their farewells and the last British soldiers took up sentry duty.

*T*hat afternoon the Civic Guards (the new unarmed police who would later be named the Garda Siochana) marched into the Castle behind Chief Superintendent McCarthy and Commissioner Michael Staines, exchanged salutes with the departing British army unit and took charge of the complex of buildings.

T he Civic Guards were soon drilling in the Castle. But not everybody was glad to see the British leave. It must have taken a fair degree of courage for these women to demonstrate their loyalties in the Dublin of 1922 as soldiers of the old regime were marching to the boat.

*N*ot surprisingly, the British soldiers themselves were glad to be on the way home. Over the months of evacuation, many happy faces were seen among the 'Tommies' at the docks as they bought fruit for the crossing or enjoyed a hot drink before embarking.

A last sing-song, and then they were gone. A more elegant vessel was later provided for General Macready at Kingstown, soon to be Dun Laoghaire.

*L*ong before the last of the British forces had left, however, the strain between the Free State authorities and the opponents of the Treaty had reached breaking-point. Meetings between leaders on both sides like (left to right) Eoin O'Duffy, Liam Lynch, Gearóid O'Sullivan and Liam Mellows came to nothing.

*W*hen the 'Republicans' (anti-Treaty I.R.A. men, called 'Irregulars' by the Provisional Government) began to occupy public buildings in Dublin, Free State soldiers held up people in the streets on suspicion and searched them.

*I*n the earlier part of the year British troops had guarded the Four Courts, the masterpiece of eighteenth century architecture which housed the courts of justice in Dublin. Republicans under Rory O'Connor (left) occupied the building in April. After two months, growing Republican audacity and British pressure provoked the Provisional Government to retake the Four Courts. When O'Connor refused to surrender, preparations were made for an artillery assault from across the river.

On 30 June, a pall of smoke rose above the city when a Free State shell hit the Irregulars' ammunition store in the Four Courts complex.

*F*ires smouldered on in the
Four Courts and further
demolition had to be
undertaken afterwards to
ensure that passers-by were
not hit by falling masonry.

The facade of the
building appeared to be
relatively intact (opposite)
but damage to the wings was
severe (opposite) — and note
the fallen tram-wires.

*T*he action now
moved down-river.
Free State soldiers
cleared Mary's
Lane. Republicans
evacuated the
Ballast Office. St
John's Ambulance
men were kept
busy tending to
civilians caught up
in the fighting
(opposite).

*D*ubliners watched in horror as gunfire again broke out in O'Connell Street, six years after Easter Week but now between an Irish state and its Irish opponents.

When this photograph was taken the Free State forces had launched an attack on the buildings occupied by Republicans adjacent to the Gresham Hotel (on the right-hand side of the street, beyond Nelson Pillar).

An intrepid priest led people in Marlborough Street, behind the Gresham Hotel, to the comparative safety of the Model Schools.

F ree State artillery reduced
the Hammam building in
O'Connell Street and the
Gresham Hotel to ruins.

    Cathal Brugha, who
had taken the Republican
side, was killed in the
attack and his body was
brought to lie in state in
the Mater Hospital.

A tragic series of funerals was to mark July and August 1922.

The first was that of Cathal Brugha, whose pall-bearers included Seán T. O'Kelly, the future President of Ireland. Among the mourners was Mary MacSwiney, sister of Terence, and Father Albert stood with the family at the graveside.

Despite the political bitterness of the Civil War divisions, Michael Collins refused to listen to personal criticism of Brugha.

Arthur Griffith died suddenly on 12 August. Although his formal office was President of the Dail, he was the principal figure after Collins on the Free State side during the intensely difficult period of transition. The Lord Lieutenant, who had not yet left Ireland, paid his respects in Dublin's Pro-Cathedral prior to the funeral.

With the outbreak of the Civil War, Collins became Commander-in-Chief of the Army with the rank of General. He attended the funeral of Arthur Griffith with other senior officers. From left, Michael Collins, Richard Mulcahy and (second behind Mulcahy on outside rank) Kevin O'Higgins.

*T*he country learned with deep shock that Michael Collins had been killed on 22 August at Béal na mBláth in his native

county of Cork. He was shot dead by a party of Republicans who ambushed the military convoy in which, apparently

unknown to them, the Commander-in-Chief was travelling. The bewildered grief of his brother, Seán, at the lying in state in

Dublin's City Hall spoke for many thousands of his fellow-citizens.

*T*he people of Dublin stood in line to pay their last respects to Michael Collins.

So too, in a chivalrous gesture, did a party of British N.C.O.s, still in the country awaiting evacuation.

*T*he gun-carriage and its escort made their
way slowly through the streets of Dublin to
Glasnevin Cemetery.

. . . 'and the little children cried in the streets.'
John Morley's lines on the death of
William the Silent could have been aptly
quoted at the funeral of Michael Collins,
where young fruitsellers shared the
country's distress.

William T. Cosgrave now became Chairman of the Provisional Government and, when the Constitution enacted under the Treaty came into effect in December, President of the Executive Council (Prime Minister) of the Irish Free State: he raised the flag on Dublin's City Hall, where he had been a prominent member of the City Council.

Cosgrave brought the Civil War to a close but imprisoned many Republicans— including Éamon de Valera, whose schoolboy son Vivion addressed a public meeting on his father's behalf.

*D*e Valera and others were held for a time in Kilmainham Jail. Much bitterness had been engendered in the later months of the Civil War by outrages on both sides, but especially by the execution of Republicans like Erskine Childers under draconian Free State legislation enacted to pacify the country. Republican women, including the socialist Madame Despard, organised a 'Release the Prisoners' fund and undertook vigils outside the jails.

As the new state became firmly established, normal life resumed. The Governor-General was Timothy Healy, who had been Parnell's main opponent at the time of the 'Split'; he went to the races and the Horse Show at Ballsbridge, where parades again took place in the jumping enclosure.

S *port of all kinds flourished in the*
Free State: clay pigeon shooting
at Clondalkin; international
swimming at the Tara Street
Baths in Dublin, where a
German girl set up records;
trying out greyhounds at the new
Shelbourne Park track; a cycle
rally in the Phoenix Park.

*T*eam events provided much of
the entertainment at the
Tailteann Games in 1924.
The parade to Croke Park
was led by two young men
with wolfhounds.

There were tug-of-war teams as well as Irish and American hurling teams at the Tailteann Games.

G ene Tunney, the world heavyweight boxing champion, (second from left) was greeted on arrival at Dun Laoghaire by General O'Duffy (left), Count John McCormack the famous tenor, and Colonel James Fitzmaurice the Army Air Corps officer who was navigator on the first transatlantic flight from east to west in 1928. Dan Breen was seen at Leopardstown Races (right) and the press photographers were kept busy at a rugby match in Lansdowne Road.

*S*ir John Lavery, the painter, and his wife Hazel, whose features would later appear as the allegorical representation of Ireland on the state's currency notes, visited the Governor-General at the former Vice-Regal Lodge. Other painters, including Jack Yeats (far right) and Leo Whelan (below right), worked in Dublin and 'AE' — George Russell — was editor of the journal The Irish Statesman.

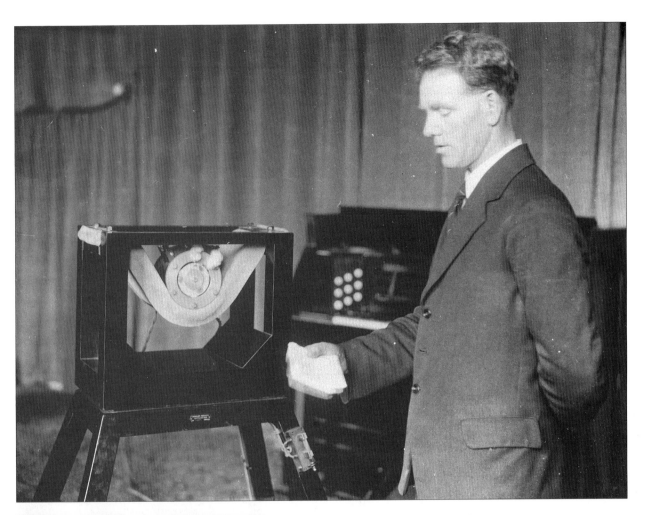

*B*roadcasting arrived in 1926 with the opening of the state radio service, 2RN, later Radio Eireann. The first announcer was Séamus Hughes (above). The first Director of Broadcasting was Séamus Clandillon (below), an authority on Irish music and a singer himself. John McCormack (front left) had, of course, the outstanding Irish voice of the day. His many distinctions included an honorary doctorate of the National University.

When veteran Fenian John Devoy came to Dublin from America he received a presentation from Seán McGarry, an I.R.B. member and supporter of the Treaty. The dapper Mayor Jimmy Walker of New York looked like a character out of Scott Fitzgerald when he signed his name to receive the freedom of the city of Kilkenny.

Princess Mary of England, later the Princess Royal, arrived at the North Wall in Dublin with her husband, Viscount Lascelles, and received a friendlier welcome than she probably expected. An especially important visit for the status of the new Irish state was that of Frank B. Kellogg, U.S. Secretary of State, in 1928. President Cosgrave received him at Dun Laoghaire (opposite), escorted him in the capital (opposite) and ensured that he was accorded every mark of respect (opposite).

*P*olitical life continued. The Anti-Treatyites began to edge their way into the system. Dan Breen was elected a T.D. in 1923, Seán Lemass in 1924. At first, like the other Republican deputies, they refused to take their seats. Éamon de Valera became increasingly convinced that abstention served no useful purpose and, when he failed to persuade Sinn Fein of this, resigned and formed his own party, Fianna Fail. At the General Election in June 1927 Fianna Fail won 44 seats in the Dail out of 153. De Valera led his party (opposite, left, Patrick J. Ruttledge, and right, Gerry Boland, behind him Countess Markievicz) into Leinster House, the seat of the Dail and Senate, but refused to take the oath of allegiance. He thereupon led his party out again (opposite, right, Seán T. O'Kelly, Ruttledge, Seán MacEntee). Diehard Republicans like Frank Ryan (opposite, unveiling a 1916 memorial at Glasnevin) refused to collaborate with de Valera in his attempt to participate in Free State politics.

William Cosgrave, a fine orator, dominated Irish politics during the first ten years of the Free State.

Attention increasingly focussed, however, on Kevin O'Higgins who was Minister for Home Affairs and later for Justice (the same portfolio) in successive cabinets. He was considered the 'strong man' of the government because of his firm commitment to law and order, symbolised in his support for the Garda Siochana.

O'Higgins found a reflection of his own stoic concept of duty in the Gardai, policemen of the new state, who died while endeavouring to enforce the law and in whose honour he unveiled a memorial.

He enjoyed relaxation from work and was to be seen with Mrs O'Higgins at Punchestown Races and the Dublin Horse Show.

W hile going to Mass on Sunday 10 July 1927, Kevin O'Higgins was shot dead by unknown gunmen in this suburban roadway at Booterstown, County Dublin. His body was carried from the Mansion House, where it had lain in state; Governor-General Healy and President Cosgrave led the funeral procession.

A *few days later the Countess Markievicz died in a Dublin hospital. Her funeral passed through Capel Street; her husband and her son came from Paris and Éamon de Valera was at the graveside.*

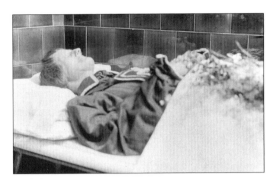

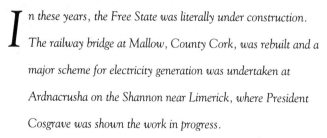

I n these years, the Free State was literally under construction. The railway bridge at Mallow, County Cork, was rebuilt and a major scheme for electricity generation was undertaken at Ardnacrusha on the Shannon near Limerick, where President Cosgrave was shown the work in progress.

A rtist Seán Keating painted the
Shannon Scheme as it evolved.

*T*he trade union leader, Jim Larkin, returned from America to a rapturous welcome in 1923. The Free State acquired a new Governor-General in 1928 — James MacNeill, a former member of the Indian Civil Service who had joined the pre-1916 Sinn Fein movement and become High Commissioner (ambassador) of the Free State in London. He is seen here with Mrs MacNeill at the former Vice-Regal Lodge. He had to leave office in 1932 when he found himself at odds with the Fianna Fail government. Dónal Ó Buachalla succeeded him.

M ajor church ceremonies took place in the Phoenix Park to celebrate the centenary of Catholic Emancipation in 1929.

Movie cameramen (foreground) were now present on such occasions.

*F*ollowing the murder of O'Higgins the government brought in legislation which would have unseated T.D.s who refused to take the oath of allegiance. De Valera yielded to the extent of allowing Fianna Fail to go through what he called the 'empty formula' of signing the register, which was accepted as sufficient compliance. Fianna Fail became the principal opposition party in the Dail and attracted growing support in the Free State — helped by the daily newspaper, the Irish Press, founded by de Valera in 1931 and edited with flair by Frank Gallagher.

After the General Election of 1932 Fianna Fail took office with the support of the Labour Party. Éamon de Valera became President of the Executive Council and was photographed outside Leinster House with his government which included men who were to give long service as Ministers, such as Frank Aiken (front row, extreme left), Dr Jim Ryan (front row, third from right), Seán MacEntee (back row, extreme left), Seán T. O'Kelly (back row, second from left) and Seán Lemass (back row, second from right).

*J*oe Cashman had photographed
O'Connell Street in Dublin on
tense and tragic occasions during
the previous twenty years but the
central boulevard of the capital
was looking its best for the
International Eucharistic
Congress in June 1932.

An altar for the
celebration of Benediction was
erected on the bridge, while a
symbolic gateway was built
beside the tramlines at the
entrance to the city on the
Merrion Road.

*T*he city itself was changing, too. It was in
1932 that the original Butt Bridge was
replaced by a modern and much wider
structure. In time the old Liberty Hall
(left centre background), which featured
in a number of Cashman news
photographs, would be succeeded by
Dublin's first high-rise building, the new
Liberty Hall which stands today on the
quayside site in the left background of
both these pictures. It houses the Dublin
regional offices of SIPTU, the major
trade union formed by the amalgamation
of the two unions founded by Jim Larkin.

HISTORIC PHOTO'S

Joe Cashman took this photograph of himself taking a photograph of himself!

And in 1966 he photographed the passers-by who stopped to look at a display of his pictures in the window of the Irish Press office in O'Connell Street.